Expect Success

How to Accomplish Anything in Life Using Your Inner Circle of Success

Drew Laughlin

Black Shirt Publishing, Omaha, NE

Expect Success

Published by
Black Shirt Publishing
www.BlackShirtPublishing.com

Printed in the United States of America

ISBN 978-0-578-00372-6

This book is available at quantity discounts for bulk purchases. For information, visit:
www.YouCanExpectSuccess.com

Visit our exciting performance improvement site at:
www.AchieveNational.com

This book is dedicated to Big Al.

Testimonials

"An insightful, illuminating book. A quick read with mind-expanding ideas."

> - **Dr. Joe Vitale**, author "The Attractor Factor"
> www.MrFire.com

"This book can help you greatly. I love Drew's no nonsense style. If you follow his instruction, you will be able to accomplish almost anything!"

> - **Zev Saftlas**, Author of "Motivation That Works",
> Founder of www.EmpoweringMessages.com

"I've been using and studying self improvement strategies for years and I must say this book is something special. Not only does it cover success factors that others use but if shows you how to implement them in your own life. Priceless!"

> - **Eva Gregory**, author of "Life Lessons for
> Mastering the Law of Attraction" and
> "The Feel Good Guide to Prosperity",
> www.LeadingEdgeCoaching.com

"A straight-to-the-point, 'this is how you do it' book that everyone should use to succeed not only professionally but personally as well. Expect results and Expect Success!"

> - **Frank Traditi**, author of "Get Hired Now!"
> www.CoachFrank.com

"This book is filled with useful tools and strategies that you can use immediately to win at the success game."

> - **Jeffrey J. Fox**, author of "How to Get to the Top"
> www. FoxandCompany.com

"This book is excellent! I really enjoyed reading it and know I'm going to use this book in my own quest for self-improvement. It will work great for sales people or anyone on a corporate level and can be helpful to people in their personal life."

       - **Dana Prince**, www.DanaPrinceWriting.com

"Drew has the gift of making complex ideas simple and you'll find them to be incredibly effective. I have been implementing Drew's ideas for years now and they work! Drew gives you a roadmap for how to focus on being more effective and if you focus on your inner circle, expect success."

       - **Greg Chambers**, www.MadGringo.com

"Part of the reason more people are not successful is that they want it to be easy, and it's usually not. Here's a book that blueprints exactly how easy it can be, if you follow the simple steps."

       - **Art Sobczak**, author of
  "How to Sell More, in Less Time, With No Rejection"
      www.BusinessByPhone.com

"This is a must read! Drew provides an easy-to-use map that guarantees success if you really want to accomplish more out of life."

       - **Marsha Petrie Sue**, MBA, CSP and author of
    "Toxic People" www. MarshaPetrieSue.com

"Ready to create your own success? Grab a highlighter and begin reading Expect Success right now - it can change your life. Read it with discipline, implement the actions with passion, and teach what you learn to others!"

       - **David Cottrell**, author of
     "Monday Morning Leadership"
    www.CornerstoneLeadership.com

"In Expect Success, Drew Laughlin highlights the difference between Outer Circle Thinking and Inner Circle Thinking. These concepts alone will give readers more life fulfillment than they've experienced in years."
- **Rich Fettke**, author of "Extreme Success"
www.Fettke.com

"Read this book and discover the power of your 'Inner Circle.' You'll find that success is not something that happens 'to you,' but rather a choice. Make that choice!"
- **Joe Calloway**, author of "Becoming A Category of One"
www.JoeCalloway.com

"Expect Success" points you in the direction and gives you the tools you need to achieve. Real world success for real world people. Buy it. Devour it. Repeat. The message is brilliant."
- **Kevin Hogan**, Psy.D., author of
"The Psychology of Persuasion"
www.KevinHogan.com

"I am a small business owner. I have grown personally and in the business world thanks to Drew Laughlin's book. It contains essential tools needed to become the true achiever you always knew you could be."
- **Richard Rochelle**, Owner,
Luckey's Quality Auto Painting
www.LuckeysQualityAutoPainting.com

"A solid success manual that can help you to move towards the achievement of your goals."
- **Tom Butler-Bowdon**, author of "50 Success Classics",
"50 Prosperity Classics"
www.Butler-Bowdon.com

"This book will make you" think". Never underestimate what you can achieve. What you expect is the first step to achieving your goals in life."

- Lee Cockerell, Executive Vice President (Retired) Walt Disney World® Resort, author of "Creating Magic...10 Common Sense Leadership Strategies from a Life at Disney" www.LeeCockerell.com

"Drew Laughlin's *Expect Success* is an absolute must read for anyone seeking simple, powerfully effective strategies to achieve success in business and in life. If you want to take your success to the next level, you need to read this book."

- Dr. Ivan Misner, NY Times Bestselling author and Founder of BNI, www.bni.com

Acknowledgments

Let me say that I would be a fool if I didn't acknowledge the people around me who made this book possible. First and foremost, there's my wonderful wife, Debbie, and my amazing kids, Taylor and Sam.

I would also like to give a shout out to everyone who stood behind me and believed that I could make this book a success. There are too many people to list here, but you know who you are.

Finally, I also want to thank everyone who didn't believe in me and thought I would never do this, much less be successful. I thank you because you were my greatest motivation!

Preface

In order to achieve success we must be able and willing to look inside ourselves instead of outside at others. Each one of us holds our own answers to success. This book is about how to find the right answers at the right time.

This book will teach you how to look inside for the skills, attitudes and knowledge to achieve all the success you can handle. It will give you a step-by-step system, a process that you can use any time and every time you want to achieve something.

It wasn't until recently that I began to achieve success at great levels. Before that, I was too focused on the things around me that I couldn't control. I was waiting for things to happen to me instead of making things happen for me. Then I started following the system in this book and it brought me immediate success.

When you discover the secrets in this book you may think that some are "obvious" or "I already do that." If so, then let me challenge you to follow the 5-step system for a month. I'm willing to bet that you'll accomplish more in the next 30 days than you have in the last few months combined!

When you finish this book you may have some questions. You'll probably feel the need to look outside for the answers. Resist the temptation. Look inside and use the 5-step system until the answers come to you. They will come to you. From that point forward you really can accomplish anything you want out of life!

To maximize the value of this book I have divided it into three modules. The first module will teach you the fundamental of success; including Inner Circle and Outer Circle Thinking.

The second module details the 15 Critical Success Factors that all successful people have and use to achieve their success. Now you can duplicate their exact habits and expect the same results.

Finally the third module explains the proven 5-step success system you can use to accomplish anything in your life. It works. You just need to use it!

To your success,

Drew Laughlin
Author, *Expect Success*

Table of Contents

Your Free Gift

Expect Success
Free Audio Presentation

Go to:

www.YouCanExpectSuccess.com/bonuses

and download a special audio training. This instantly downloadable MP3 is free to you for trusting me to help you achieve success faster than you ever thought possible.

Thank you.

Module I

Understanding the Fundamentals of Success

1

Introduction

"Success seems to be largely a matter of hanging on after others have let go."

William Feather

You're about to discover the most important rule of success. It's called the Inner Circle of Success (ICS). Once you understand this rule, you'll be able to take control of every aspect of your life and achieve the success you desire.

You'll never have to worry or wait for someone else to help you be successful. You'll finally be able to control your destiny. People will begin to look up to you as a role model. People will want to be around you and show you the respect that you deserve. The status quo will no longer be acceptable to you.

When you've completed this book, you'll be able to look in the mirror and say to yourself, "I know exactly what I need to do to achieve all the success I can possibly handle."

This Book Is Perfect for You If...

This book is perfect for you if you're struggling to stay above water in a sea of discontent, overwhelm, or confusion as to who you are, what you want to be, and how to get where you want to go. If you want to achieve success at a high level and maintain it forever, keep reading.

Stay with me if you're looking for proven, reproducible methods and strategies to achieve consistent success. Everything we're going to discuss has been field-tested and approved by some of the most successful people on earth. Use these methods and you just might become as successful and fulfilled as them.

For the last several years, my team and I have researched and studied specific success factors. It wouldn't surprise me if you can guess what most of these traits and characteristics are. But you may be surprised at how few people achieve the success they want and desire, even when they have a general, though fuzzy, idea of how to get there.

What's the difference between those who get what they want and those who don't? It's all about a single-minded, intense focus combined with variety of specific, proven success habits you'll need to achieve the results you desire.

That's what this book is all about: helping you understand what these Critical Success Factors are and how to use them so you can become one of the few who get where they're going and experience the success they deserve.

How to Get the Most out of this Book

The simplest way to get the most benefit out of anything you do is repetition. Doing something over and over again makes it easier to understand, and you become more efficient at that task. Using the contents of this book is no different.

It's like learning to play guitar. When you first pick up the instrument, you can barely produce a single clear note. Even if someone shows you how to play a chord, it probably won't sound very good at first.

But when you play that same chord over and over again, it begins to sound like music!

Read this book at least two to three times before you begin any of the action steps. It's important to gain a complete, high-level understanding of all the contents before attempting to master any one skill.

At this time, you may not be clear on where you would like to improve the most. Therefore, it's important to make a plan first and then implement the plan. You can't do that until you read through this entire book at least a couple times.

Your Biggest Obstacles to Success

If you're reading this book, it's likely that you are not achieving the success you want or feel you deserve. That's okay! You can admit it. Believe me, you're not alone.

On the other hand, perhaps you're very successful and simply want to keep your edge. Maybe you even want to gain an additional advantage. No wonder you're reading this book!

The reason many people struggle to achieve the success they desire comes down to lacking three simple things: they don't possess the knowledge, skills, and attitudes they need to obtain the achievements they crave.

If this is you, I say again, you're not alone! If everyone knew what to do and how to do it, everyone would be hugely successful. And how fun would that be?

It's also not necessarily all your fault. Considering that less than three percent of us truly achieve the success we desire, it's clear that almost no one knows the secrets. Those who don't have probably followed the wrong advice, don't have the discipline to follow through, or merely dream of success while actually sabotaging themselves, preventing themselves from ever achieving their goals.

The good thing, there *is* a better way.

How to Achieve Success

Let's say I really know soccer, and I show you the proper way to kick a soccer ball. If you practice the correct technique over and over again, can you expect to kick a soccer ball at an exceptional level? Of course you can. Even if you're not as strong as someone else, you can still expect results similar to those of someone who has been playing soccer for years.

Granted, everyone is different, and you may not be able to kick a soccer ball as far as a pro can. But at the same time, you may be able to kick it farther and more accurately than someone who has been playing soccer her whole life if you've been better trained, even if you only practice for a short period of time.

It all comes down to know-how, effort, and a willingness to get better. The success secrets we are going to cover in this book are no different. You can achieve greater success – perhaps greater than those who have been training for years – if you apply the secrets you'll find here.

Why this Book Is Different

This book follows its own advice. It's not loaded with a bunch of fluff and filler content. It gets straight to the point and shows you how to implement the strategies, principles, and tactics inside immediately.

As I stated before, we have done a lot of research and study on the various ways people become successful. This book is a concise and focused approach to outlining exactly what other successful people do and how you can duplicate their exact strategies, traits, and characteristics.

By reading this book and using the 15 Critical Success Factors inside, you can expect the same results as the most successful people anywhere in the world. Learn these fifteen success factors. Master them. You'll gain tremendous empowerment, energy, and education on how you can increase your performance and happiness immediately.

Let me warn you: these aren't simply theories to read and eventually forget. Rather, they are practical tools you can put to work immediately and repeat daily to enhance your life, both professionally and personally.

What Is the Inner Circle of Success?

Most people who read this book or attend our seminars and workshops have no clue that the Inner Circle of Success even exists, much less how to apply it to their own lives.

While you may be able to guess what some of the Success Factors are, you need to know how to use them in a way that will work for you. First, though, let's go over what the Inner Circle of Success really is.

How Our Outer Circle and Inner Circle Work Together

Everything we do can be placed into just two Success Circles: the Outer Circle and the Inner Circle. That's it – every move you make belongs in one or the other, and if you really want to succeed, you need to fill up the Inner Circle faster than the Outer.

The Outer Circle contains everything that happens outside your control. How the company you work for makes decisions sits in the outer circle. How your colleagues choose to behave is there, too. The yahoo who runs the red light and almost hits your brand new car? Outer Circle, for sure. These are all examples of events that happen in your outer circle, out of your hands and beyond your control.

In contrast, the Inner Circle consists of everything you *can* control. What you can control are the decisions you make and your mindset towards those decisions. And how do you gain this control, this mastery of the Inner Circle? You take charge of your Inner Circle with the 15 Critical Success Factors and implement the 5-step system you'll soon learn.

We Focus Too Much on Our Outer Circle

It's not really our fault, but as humans, we tend to focus on events outside our control. It's just the way things are. Isn't it easier to blame the economy, our bosses, our spouses, or the government when things aren't going the way we feel they should? Of course. We all do it – or at least we have done it at one time in our lives.

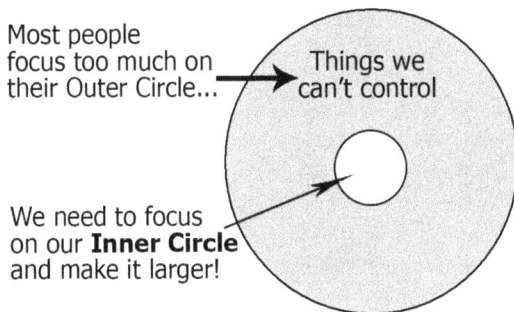

Most people focus too much on their Outer Circle...
→ Things we can't control

We need to focus on our **Inner Circle** and make it larger!

When you choose to focus on your Outer Circle instead of your Inner Circle, you immediately set yourself up to fail. It's impossible to achieve success when you're worried about what everyone else is doing or blaming others for the things that happen in your life.

Now, I am a firm believer in knowledge, education, and training; however, most people don't need more job training to make a dramatic difference in their success levels.   Let's take sales training, for example. So many sales people blame their training for a lack of results because it's an easy out. They'll insist on getting more training so they can do their jobs better or they'll insist on getting new "tools" to help them.

The bottom line is they don't need these tools or additional training. They have enough! What's really holding them back is simply their focus on the wrong circle.

Take This 'OCT' Quiz

Following is a simple ten question quiz. It will help you understand and identify the level of Outer Circle Thinking (OCT) you do. By simply reading these statements aloud you will recognize instantly where Outer Circle thinking is holding you back.

Simply put a checkmark in the box next to each statement that you've said in the last ninety days. Please understand that if you said a statement that is somewhat close to the one listed but not exact be sure to checkmark that box.

Which statements below have you said in the last ninety days?

☐ "If fast food didn't taste so good I could lose weight."

☐ "They don't have a clue what goes on out here in the field."

☐ "If the gym was closer to my house I would work out all the time."

☐ "If my wife/husband was nicer to me I'd be nicer to her/him."

☐ "If my boss would give me a new laptop I'd make more sales."

☐   "Why would I help them, it's not my job."

☐   "You never listen to me."

☐   "That stuff never works."

☐   "I smoke because <u>you / my work / my boss</u> stress me out."

☐   "I'm sorry I can't help you that's against our policy."

How did you do? If you checked even one statement you partake in Outer Circle Thinking. If you checked more than one statement then congratulations! You're human!

We Need Our Outer Circle, but not as much as We Think

At first, when someone doesn't understand the concept of Outer Circle Thinking versus Inner Circle Thinking, they come to me and say, "I have to have an Outer Circle or I can't pay the bills." I respond with, "You're absolutely correct! However, just because everyone needs an Outer Circle doesn't mean they have to depend on their Outer Circle to be successful."

Sometimes my response helps them understand. Other times I launch into what the rest of this book is about and then, inevitably, they get it.

Everyone needs an Outer Circle of Success. The problem lies when we depend on it too much. Or we choose to blame our problems on our Outer Circle instead of looking inside.

Things like our job, the people we work with and the friends we choose to be around are all examples of our Outer Circle. We need them. But we all control our own thinking and the choices we make. No one else can do that for us. That's why true success lives in our Inner Circle.

Success Lives in Our Inner Circle

If you're honest with yourself, you'll probably find you need to change your mindset and focus on your Inner Circle using the 15 Critical Success Factors we'll be covering in this book. And as a reward for that honesty, success will pour down on you like a hurricane in a rainforest.

Perhaps Yogi Berra said it best: *"Baseball is 90 percent mental – the other half is physical."* While Yogi's math may be off, his point is right on. In sports, business, or life in general, 90 percent of our success is determined by our mental strength, or Inner Circle. The other half – or ten percent, if your math's a little better – is the amount that depends on your Outer Circle.

This is what our **Inner Circle** should look like....

A perfect 90/10 ratio!

Focus on the things we can control...

The 15 Critical Success Factors!

While we must have an Outer Circle to be successful, it's never as important as our Inner Circle.

How big is your Inner Circle compared to your Outer Circle? If you don't have a 90/10 ratio, keep reading.

One more thing before we get started: read the statement below as many times as needed until it sticks and you're ready to move forward with an open, clear mind. Always remember:

**"The mind is like a parachute.
It's best used when open!"**

Module II

15 Critical Success Factors that Make Up Your Inner Circle of Success

2

The Success Wheel

If you would, imagine a wagon wheel from the Old West. One where in the middle is the hub and attached to the hub are fourteen spokes that are spread out evenly to make the wheel a perfect circle.

Of the fourteen spokes, each one is as equally important as all the others. However, the hub is special. Without the hub it is impossible to have a wheel. It would simply crumble to the ground because there would be nothing to hold the spokes in place. There would be nothing to support the wheel as a whole.

As you read through the next 15 Critical Success Factors you'll begin to understand why each one is vital to your success. But don't try to figure out how the success wheel should look. Don't worry about which one is the hub and which ones are the spokes.

The wheel will be completed for you at the end of this section. For now, simply read and understand where, how and why these success factors are important in your life.

The Success Wheel

Belief

"We can achieve what we can conceive and believe."

Mark Twain

One of the things that the majority of people find most challenging about success is sincere, unshakable belief, not just in themselves but also in their companies and their products.

When you believe, you give yourself the power to accomplish anything you desire. You're no longer at the mercy of hoping and wishing for something good to happen. When you focus and believe in the right things, you *make* good things happen.

Believe in Yourself

Let's start by focusing on you. Whether you like it or not, your beliefs dictate your behavior. Too often, we do not behave in a way that serves our best interests; our behavior becomes self defeating because we believe that we can't do something.

What it boils down to is a slew of limiting beliefs that we have about ourselves. These limiting beliefs then undermine the knowledge and confidence we have in our products, the way we communicate with customers and colleagues, and even our ability to perform at an optimum level.

Let's take this book as an example: I wrote this book, the core of it, more than two years ago; however, I was sabotaging myself at the same time. I was telling myself, "The content is good but it's not good enough. No one will read it. If someone *does* read it, they won't like it."

This is a perfect example of limiting beliefs. For a long time, they put a stranglehold on me, but then I was finally able to break through. Just think, if I didn't eliminate these false beliefs, I wouldn't be able to help the hundreds of people that I do today. What a bummer that would be – both for me and for them.

If you honestly and critically analyze your beliefs about what you can or cannot do, chances are you're dominated by limiting beliefs that are holding you back. To break through, like I did, you need to get rid of those limiting beliefs.

Eliminate Limiting Beliefs

It goes back to a saying your mother or father likely told you on more than one occasion: "You can do anything you set your mind to."

That, in and of itself, is a very truthful, very powerful statement. You really *can* do anything you put your mind to. If you look back through history, you'll see that many successful people had to overcome limiting beliefs to achieve the successes we remember them for.

As you read earlier, I'm a perfect example. Those who achieve success can look back and realize that old saying is amazingly accurate. You really can do anything you set your mind to.

It's a matter of burying those unwanted, "I can't do it" beliefs with an avalanche of positive, "I *can* do it!" beliefs. The bottom line is you are smart enough to achieve your goals, both professionally and personally. Isn't it about time you started believing that, too?

Believe in Your Company

You need to have complete confidence that your product, service, and company are the right fit for you. If you have any doubts about your company or your product, you're going to have a very difficult time succeeding on a professional level.

You're going to feel like you're doing your customers, colleagues, and even yourself a disservice. Even worse, you may feel you're lying to your customers because you don't believe that your product is the best option available.

> **Did You Know?**
>
> It's not enough to believe in yourself. You must be willing to believe in the company you work for and the products you represent.

To build your belief in your product, you must have a deep knowledge of the product. You need to clearly understand all its limitations, as well as the features and benefits it offers.

The same goes for your company: if you're not providing the level of customer service you feel you should, the strength of your beliefs in your organization is going to be limited. You must find ways to overcome these limits. If you can't do that, the next option is to work for a company you can believe in. The bottom line is that you must be willing and able to support your company without hesitation.

Now Take Action

Identify your limiting beliefs, those success killers that are holding you back. Make a focused effort to eliminate one unwanted belief by simply stating it the opposite way. For example, instead of saying to yourself, "I can't play guitar," say "I can and I will play guitar." And keep saying that to yourself until it becomes real!

If you are struggling with belief in your company and/or products, identify the reasons why and then make a plan to change those beliefs. If needed, seek help from a superior. Believe it or not, they are often very willing to help.

Effort

"Do or do not. There is no try."

Yoda

One thing almost everyone forgets about success is that it takes effort. As human beings, we are always looking for the fast and easy fix, the "get rich quick" idea that will finally end all of our financial problems.

Fortunately, the world doesn't work like that. To be successful, you must apply focused, sustained effort in pursuit of your goals.

Definition of Effort

Effort means consistently doing the right things at the right times.

If you consistently put forth a great effort, you're going to ensure your success. But you must determine the right things to do and the right times to do them.

If you're a salesperson, for example, you may have put great effort into researching ideas or sending out emails. However, if you're doing this during selling time – when you should be focusing on revenue producing activities, like face-to-face sales calls, presentations, and follow up – you're not doing the right thing at the right time.

You need to focus your effort where it will do the most good, at the time it will do the most good. Do your revenue producing activities during selling time. Resist the temptation to do the "fun" things before the most important things.

Be Willing to Take on the Tough Tasks

It is our nature to gravitate towards the things we like to do. But to be successful, we must be willing to do the things that others won't. That mindset alone will separate us from our competition. You can bet the farm that your competitors are not doing the tough tasks.

Doing the right activities at the right time with a focused effort is going to ensure your success – maybe more than anything else.

To achieve greatness, always put forth a strong effort toward your goals. Without effort, greatness is rarely achieved.

Now Take Action

Determine and list out the most important activities in your current role. Be sure to prioritize your list based on what's most important instead of what's easy or fun.

Focus on your top priorities for one week. Re-evaluate after the week's over to see where you are and how much more you've accomplished.

Listening and Communicating

"I know that you believe you understand what you think I said, but I'm not sure you realize that what you heard is not what I meant."

Robert McCloskey

A common misunderstanding people have is how communication really works.

Did You Know?

Effective communication starts with understanding the other person first.

Let me repeat the above statement: effective communication starts with understanding the other person, *first*. It does not start by insisting the other person understands you.

You must put yourself in the other person's shoes – whether it's a customer, colleague, significant other, or spouse. Your focus must be completely on the person with whom you are speaking. Put yourself in his shoes and take a genuine interest in what he or she is saying.

The #1 Key to Effective Communication

The key to effective communication is listening. And the key to listening is, quite frankly, to shut up. We must ask quality, high-gain questions of the person we're speaking with and then intently listen to every word she says. Really focus on every word, rather than thinking about what you're going to say next.

If you can master that – which is certainly easier said than done – you will master the listening skills that all effective communicators possess. Be open, honest, and have a genuine interest in the other person.

Now Take Action

For the next week, journal your conversations. Maintain a strong focus on shutting up, listening, and taking a genuine interest in the other person. After each conversation, note how much more clearly you've understood the other person.

Managing Expectations

"We tend to live up to our expectations."

Earl Nightingale

One thing that almost no one knows about success, especially when working with others, is how to manage expectations. When expectations are clearly defined and then managed, people respond better. They get the job done faster, and they normally get the job done right the first time. In short, they behave in the ways you want them to. The result is a win-win for everyone.

Allow me to give you a quick tip for parents of young children (it's an important illustration, even if you don't have kids): when you go into a store like Target or Wal-Mart, your children may throw a fit because they want a toy. When that happens, it's very embarrassing.

One thing I learned very early on was to manage my son's expectations. For example, I quickly learned that when I took my son to a store, before we even went through the front door, it was best to tell him what to expect. I managed his expectations. If I was willing to buy a small toy, I would explain to him that he had the opportunity to receive one gift while we were there.

But if I wasn't willing to do that, I would simply tell him, "Daddy has to get a couple of things, and we're going to be in and out very quickly. We're not going to get you anything today."

Systematize Your Efforts

It's amazing how effective that system is. I call it a system because you can use it systematically and it works. One time, I told my son he could have a single toy, and we then spent 20 to 30 minutes going up and down the toy aisles.

My son would pick a toy that he wanted. Then, managing his expectations, I'd clearly state that the one he chose was the only toy he was getting. He would then see another toy and put the original one back in order to get the new one. His expectations matched mine. It worked very effectively. There was never any conflict. There were no tirades or tantrums because I was able to effectively manage his expectations. Try that with your own children, and see what happens. It works!

What does this have to do with managing customers and colleagues on a professional level? When we can manage a customer's expectations of what we can or can't do and what we can or can't deliver, we're going to build a very strong relationship with that customer, even if what we say sometimes may not be exactly what she wants to hear.

When managing expectations, we need to be very clear about the expectations up front. An effective way to confirm those expectations is to follow these two steps:

> **Quick Tip**
>
> When you set clear expectations and manage to those expectations, behavior changes... in a good way!

Repeat and summarize what you communicated. This is important because you want to make sure that what you said is exactly what the other person heard. *"Per our discussion, we can complete this project by February 15, but not January 15th."*

You also need to check for agreement and understanding. "Is that still acceptable? Do you have any questions or concerns you'd like to discuss now?"

In addition, you want to be flexible when circumstances change. When circumstances do change, communicate those changes immediately. When a projected delivery date needs to be postponed, for instance, the longer we neglect to tell our customer about the changes, the more the relationship is going to suffer. If we can communicate the changes immediately, even if it's not what the customer wants to hear, we're going to ensure that we're doing right by the customer. It will also help build a stronger relationship because the customer knows that it takes guts to tell them news that is less than good.

Now Take Action

Next time you need something done a certain way, take the time to clearly explain what's expected from the person you're working with and then manage those expectations. Then, observe how quickly and efficiently the task gets done.

Goal Setting and Achievement

"A goal without a plan is just a wish."

Larry Elder

An effective way to speed up your results and achieve success faster is to set goals. Goals are so important because you must have a purpose to drive you. Aimlessly going through life without goals is the surest road to mediocrity.

There must be something you're willing to go after and willing to achieve, something that's going to drive you toward success. When you put your goals in writing, whether handwritten or on your computer, you're going to accomplish more than 97 percent of your peers.

Write it Down!

Only three percent of all people – and all of those are top performers – actually write down their goals. A goal becomes real the moment it's written down, making that written document very powerful. If the goal is only in your mind and you don't have a plan for accomplishing that goal, the likelihood of actually achieving it drops dramatically.

Goals help you accomplish the most you possibly can and help maximize your success. With a properly written goal and a plan to get there, you'll discover that even the toughest goals become realistic. But when goals are not written, they seem overwhelming and unrealistic and you may not have the guts to go after them.

Did You Know?

A goal becomes real once it's written. Writing down your goals and your plans will increase the likelihood of your being able to reach those goals.

We have a complete goal setting and achievement course on our website, but for now I'm going to give you a six-step plan to help you jump start your goal setting and success.

Six Steps to Successful Goal Setting and Achievement

The first step is to determine exactly what you want and to write it down. You need to be very specific and make your results measurable.

Next, you must establish a deadline for your goal. It can be short term, medium term, or long term. Short term goals are goals you expect to achieve in the next three to six months. The goals you'll reach in six to 12 months are medium term, and long term goals will typically take 12 months or more to achieve.

The third step is to list everything you will need to do to accomplish your goal. This list will likely expand as you proceed toward your goal. Just remember that you can always add to it, so when devising this list initially, don't get bogged down in all the minor details. Just write down what you think you will need to do to achieve your goal.

Once your list is complete, the fourth step is to prioritize the activities into a step-by-step plan.

The fifth step is to do something immediately to take action on your plan.

The sixth and final step is to track your progress daily. Be sure that you do something every day that brings you closer to your goal.

Steps five and six are so important because they call for immediate action. Do something right now. If you have a goal and you do something every day to attain it, you're going to gain a sense of accomplishment and fulfillment. You will see measurable progress that's closer to that goal than you ever were before.

It's vitally important to have goals, and it's equally important to have a quality plan to reach those goals. Follow these six steps, and you'll reach success a lot faster than 97 percent of all other people.

Now Take Action

Following the six-steps above, write out a plan to achieve one goal. Make it a short term goal that you can attain quickly. Now, follow the six steps until you achieve that goal. Once you hit the finish line, embrace the feeling of success!

Consistent Persistence

"Persistence is the twin sister of excellence. One is a matter of quality; the other, a matter of time."

Anonymous

Overachievers are successful people. Overachievement comes from consistently doing the things other people hate to do. Persist in the pursuit of your goals by doing the things others won't, and you'll reach the pinnacle of your field. You'll attain ultimate success. You'll also avoid the roller coaster that so many professionals find themselves on when they start their careers and often continue on throughout their entire professional lives.

Do what Others Hate to Do

Let's take the example of a sales professional once again. You can avoid the roller coaster ride that often comes along with revenue producing activities like cold calling, for instance. If you cold call consistently, not just when you feel like it, you'll be more successful. If you consistently cold call according to a plan, you can schedule a part of your day to focus on your cold calling efforts. In turn, you will do something that everybody else hates to do and what most people won't do on a consistent basis. Therefore, you will have a tremendous competitive advantage over all those people who won't cold call.

Consistent persistence is one of the keys that has helped so many people reach definitive success in their fields. I can't reiterate this concept enough: if you can do something

> **Quick Tip**
>
> Consistently doing the things that others hate to do is a surefire, guaranteed way to become successful in your field.

consistently, even if you don't do it very well, you're going to see results.

Way too often, people do not do the activities they should be doing on a consistent basis; they simply do them every once in a while. They don't schedule those critical activities. They just do them whenever they think about them. And that is a recipe for disaster. If you can persistently and consistently do the things you need to do to succeed, you will achieve ultimate success.

Many professionals have a list of things that rarely (if ever) get done on a timely basis (cold calling, paperwork, filing, etc.) so they go about their day feeling a mounting dread at that building pile of to-do items that's on the back burner. If you get the dreaded tasks out of the way early, your day can progressively improve instead of progressively worsen.

Now Take Action

Make a list of dreaded activities that you and everyone else in your field hate to do but that are important to your success.

Prioritize your list.

Choose the first item on your list, then make a plan and consistently do that activity until you begin to see its rewards. Then, do it some more!

Building Strong Relationships

"The glue that holds all relationships together – including the relationship between the leader and the led – is trust, and trust is based on integrity."

Brian Tracy

You might have guessed by now that I'm a sales guy at heart. I truly believe that nothing happens until something is sold. Some may argue that point, and that's fine. But I would argue back that all of us, no matter how we spend our work days, are really in sales. No matter what your job, role, or position in your company, you're a representative of that organization. Therefore, you're in sales by default. That's not a bad thing. Embrace it as fact.

What in the world does this have to do with building strong relationships? Everything. Sales and success in general are built on strong relationships.

A positive relationship can win you a lot of business. It's no secret. Even if your price is higher, if you have a strong customer relationship, price is rarely the deciding factor. When you develop a good relationship where trust and rapport is strong, the pressure of the sales process often diminishes considerably. And to build strong relationships, you need to remember just four simple keys.

Four Keys to Strong Relationships

There are four keys to strong relationships:

1. Attitude

2. Questions

3. Reliability

4. Continuous Engagement

First, your attitude towards the relationship is important. Why are you in this relationship? I'm not talking about the benefits you're going to get out of it, but why you're trying to build a relationship with a customer in the first place. What problems can you solve for him and his organization? Your mind should be on what's in it for your customer and how you are going to make him better at what he does.

The next key is the questions you ask. By asking good, high-gain questions, you're going to make the building process easier with the information you gather. You're also going to open the other person's mind so that he understands his situation better than ever before.

The third key element is reliability. Can your customers trust you to do what you say? When you say you're going to call at 3:00 p.m. on Thursday, do you call at 3:00 p.m. on Thursday – or do you have an excuse as to why you can't call? Do you push off meetings or do you hold them as advertised? When you have meetings with customers, do you actually bring more to the table than they anticipated?

The final key is continuous engagement. After you have a customer, continue to cultivate that relationship by offering quality customer service and additional ways to help the customer do his job. You want to recommend other resources and companies that can help your customers achieve their goals.

Being someone a client can turn to – being the "go to" person – will dramatically increase the effectiveness of your relationship. You do that by becoming a product, industry, and competitor expert. Don't just become an expert on your own company; become an expert on your customer's company – and industry – as well. Provide insight and knowledge about the customer's industry and you'll continue to strengthen that relationship.

Being genuine in your efforts to build positive relationships goes a long way. Customers, and anyone else you're trying to build a relationship with, will be able to identify very quickly if you're a fake.

Be willing to walk away from potential business. If your solution is not the right fit for that customer or prospect, you need to be willing to walk away and offer other potential solutions. To build the ultimate relationship, you must make the customer not only number one, not only number two, but also number three.

Did You Know?

You must be willing to walk away from business to be successful. Not everyone has to be your customer. There are good fits and bad fits. Choose the right fit for you.

Another thing to consider is that you don't always find a customer that is a perfect fit. You must be willing to walk away from potential business. If it makes sense and it's an appropriate option for your customers, refer them to an alternate solution. When you're willing to do that, you can't help but strengthen your relationships with them. It may mean that you have to give up a sale in the immediate future. However, in the long term, you'll continue to grow those bonds and, in turn, enjoy more profitable relationships in the long term.

Now Take Action

Based on the four keys discussed above, make a plan to improve one relationship. Once you work your plan you will reap the rewards of a prosperous relationship.

Organizational Skills

"The secret of all victory lies in the organization of the non-obvious."

Marcus Aurelius

Statistics prove that people lose a minimum of one hour of productivity each day to disorganization. Add that up over a year, and that's a ton of time you spend going through your desk, looking for things, and just dealing with disorganization in general.

A messy desk is a clear sign of disorganization. Anybody who says it's an "organized mess" is fooling himself. If you can clean your desk, organize your computer and put things away in an organized fashion so that they're available at either a click of a mouse or by opening a drawer, you're going to be a lot more productive.

A further sign of disorganization is procrastination, especially when it makes you reactive instead of proactive. Being reactive is another way to lose hours of productivity. If you don't have time to do things on a proactive basis because you're disorganized, you're losing valuable time. Those who say, "I don't have enough time" are kidding no one.

We've all used the "lack of time" excuse before. The bottom line is that there are people who are very, very successful, and they seem to get so much more done in a day's time than everyone around them. They work the same number of hours we do. However, they are able to get much more done because they have effective organizational skills. Eliminate the excuse of "I don't have enough time." There's always enough time. It's how you choose to spend your time that really counts.

Whenever you feel overwhelmed and out of control, take ten minutes and organize your surroundings. It will make a world of difference!

> **Quick Tip**
>
> Eliminate the "I don't have time" excuse from your vocabulary and say, "How can I make time?"

Separate Urgent from Important

Another sign of disorganization is not being able to separate urgent tasks from important tasks and important tasks from normal, everyday tasks. Some of that stems from email and voicemail. When we receive an email, we feel the need to immediately respond. In reality, that email may not need a response at all. It certainly doesn't need a response until after the urgent tasks are completed. Handling non-urgent tasks can distract you considerably and increase your stress while reducing your productivity. Handle urgent tasks, then dreaded tasks, and then work down your list based on priority.

Work from a List

The first thing you must do to become more organized is work from a list on a daily basis. You can use a Day-Timer or a calendar management software program, like Microsoft's Outlook, to accomplish this. Outlook, for example, allows you to organize your tasks based on the ABC or 1 through 5 method for prioritizing tasks.

The bottom line is that you can develop your list of tasks for each day, prioritize them, and then associate a letter or a number to help you identify what tasks you need to work on first. Don't move onto the second item until the first one is completed. Then, when the most important task is completed, move on to number two or item B. When that one's completed, you can move down the list. By following this system, you are certain to be more productive.

Plan Your Day in Advance

A key to helping you become extremely organized is to plan your day in advance, preferably the night before. When you wait until the morning to plan your day, you'll usually find it's more difficult.

There's a little more disorganization and productivity lost early in your day because various things happen in the morning, things that take away your ability to properly plan your day. By planning your day the night before, you come in the next morning ready to hit priority number one.

Imagine, for a second, how much more productive you're going to be. When you're organized and have everything

Fun Fact

Organization eliminates chaos!

moving in the right direction, you'll eliminate stress! You'll eliminate chaos! And you'll take advantage of that by turning previously wasted and unused energy into productivity.

Everyone's different, and everyone has a different opinion of his level of organization; however, you need to develop an organizational system that's going to work for you and help you be more productive.

When you develop a system, stick to it. Don't do it just once in a while; do it every day.

Now Take Action

For the next week, plan the next day's activities before you leave work. Every night for the next five working days, plan your day in advance and see how much more productive you are. The same professional principles can be applied to your personal life as well. Organize the next day's activities before you go to bed. This will help you sleep better at night (and avoid the twenty minutes of tossing and turning because you're thinking through your to-do list) and will help you to get more done each day.

Self Esteem

"Your chances of success in any undertaking can always be measured by your belief in yourself."

Robert Collier

The one life lesson I wish I had learned years ago is how having strong self-esteem is one of the most important gifts you can give yourself. Self doubt is a heavy burden that no one should carry. When your self esteem is high and you truly believe in your abilities, great things happen.

Self esteem is the value you put on yourself; it's what you see when you look in the mirror. Developing good self esteem and being proud of what you do are key success factors in your career and your life.

One thing that almost no one realizes is that you can build self esteem by having a strong work ethic. When you

> **Quick Tip**
>
> Strong work ethic = strong self esteem

work hard for the things you want, your energy, pride, and self worth skyrocket.

An example that comes to mind is your first day at a new job. There are so many things to learn and do before you can do your job well. If you're like most people, you might feel inadequate or lacking the skills you need to be successful. Your confidence and self-esteem are probably at very low levels.

As time goes on and you work your tail off to get better your performance will continue to improve. You begin to receive recognition for a job well done. And if you have a good manager, she goes out of her way to tell you how good you're doing.

Good Managers Help Build Self-Esteem

Good managers know how important it is to keep your self esteem levels high. With high self esteem, you're able to easily and independently complete tasks that once required assistance. Your confidence is at an all-time high and your self esteem is through the roof. Now you're the "go-to" person your colleagues seek out to get things done!

Believe you deserve good things. Be disciplined in your efforts when striving to reach your goals. Have confidence. Hold your chin up high and your shoulders back. Be willing to take risks and do what you know you're capable of doing because you deserve the ultimate success. You deserve to achieve your goals. All it takes is belief, a strong work ethic, and discipline to get you there.

Now Take Action

A quick way to build self esteem is to do something you love and that you're good at. Nothing boosts self belief quicker than doing something fun, especially when you're good at it. Go have some fun, put a smile on your face, and feel good about yourself!

Discipline

"Discipline is the bridge between goals and accomplishment."

Jim Rohn

Discipline is the art of controlling your own behavior and making yourself do what you need to do to be successful. To be most productive, discipline must come from within. You must have a clear understanding of what your true goals and wants are. This alone will help you discipline yourself to achieve those goals.

If your goals are unclear or if they don't reflect what you really want, discipline suffers. And when discipline suffers, you'll find it difficult to do what other people won't, one of the keys to lasting success. To hold onto the discipline that will allow you to be truly successful, you have to be willing to do what other people won't. We talked about this earlier, but it's worth repeating.

You Must Have Clear Goals

Discipline is difficult. Sometimes, our lack of self discipline steers us away from what we have to do and what we know we should be doing. Maybe those tasks are hard work. They're risky. We're afraid – maybe we're afraid to fail.

When we experience obstacles like those just mentioned, we need to understand that the reason they exist in the first place is most likely that we don't have a clear understanding of what our true goals are. That's an indication that we may need to reevaluate what we really want to do and accomplish.

Think for a second. If we lack the self discipline to accomplish something we really want, then how bad do we really want it?

Did You Know?

For many, it's easier to get up at 5:00 a.m. on Saturday to go golfing then it is to get up at noon on Monday to go to work!

Let's use golf and work to illustrate my point. Years ago, I was working in a job that I didn't like. At the time, I would need to get up at five o'clock in the morning – very early for most people. Even though

I'm a morning person, I still had trouble getting up. You see, I didn't like my job, so the discipline I needed to get to work on time was very weak. I didn't want to go, so I would show up just before I would be considered late.

But golfing at 5:00 a.m. on Saturday? No problem. Why was it so easy to get up at 5:00 a.m. on a Saturday morning to go golfing when I could barely get out of bed to go to work? Because I didn't like work. I wasn't having fun.

That's when I knew I had to change careers. Now, I conduct corporate training, coach others to success, and provide success products to a market that wants to improve their lives. And guess what? I have absolutely no problem getting up in the morning! I love what I do and it shows. It's amazing how much discipline we have when we're doing something we enjoy.

Create Discipline

Perhaps you're in a position where you can't go out and do something you love because you need to pay the bills. I get that. What you need to do to produce discipline is to create a fun and enjoyable work environment.

There was a company I worked with that had all its cubicles set up so that the desks were facing toward the window. Sounds nice, right? Employees looked out the window instead of at a wall. However, the reality of the situation was that when someone walked through the office, those sitting at their desks had their backs turned to them.

This was not very inviting, to say the least. One woman who was struggling with the way things were going suggested turning all the desks around so that the employees would face out and have their backs at the window. This created an immediate change in the culture of their work environment, making it much more inviting and open. Teamwork improved. People enjoyed being around each other more. And everyone was much more productive.

Now, the woman who was once struggling with discipline is no longer struggling! She's excelling!

Now Take Action

Conduct a quick self evaluation to see where you may lack discipline in your life. Focus on one area and create discipline by making your environment fun and inviting.

Motivation and Desire

"People often say that motivation doesn't last. Well, neither does bathing – that's why we recommend it daily."

Zig Ziglar

Motivation is the driving force from within that causes an individual to act in order to achieve a specific goal. In short, the want has to be stronger than the process. What does that mean? Well, let's take a sales goal, for example.

You want to reach a specific income level. In order to do that, you have figured out that you need to make 25 cold calls a day. That's part of the process. Maybe you need to go to a certain number of networking meetings. Maybe you need to attend a certain number of prospecting events. Maybe you need to meet with a certain number of customers.

That's what you need to do. But do you want to do it? Are you motivated to do what you need to do to go where you want to go?

The Want Must Be Stronger than the Process

The "want" or ultimate goal has to be stronger than the process it takes to get there. Let's say that all you do is focus on how you need to make 25 cold calls today. You're thinking to yourself, "I'm not really up for it. I'll do something else." That means the process is outweighing the want. It's heavier than the want, and you're not going to achieve your goal.

When you are developing goals and you're looking for that inner motivation, your desire to achieve that goal has to more powerful than the process it takes to get there. Take Tiger Woods, for instance. His desire to be the greatest golfer of all time is so strong that it creates its own momentum. He is so intense about his goals that motivation and desire aren't even an issue. It's like someone needs to invent new words because Tiger's off the charts when it comes to motivation.

Whenever anybody has a conversation about the greatest golfers of all time, they inevitably mention Tiger Woods. Everybody else is an afterthought, including greats like Jack Nicklaus. That want is so strong for Tiger that the process to get there is insignificant to him.

Tiger puts in many hours of grueling training and practices smacking golf balls over and over again. He rehearses the same shot repeatedly. He shows up on the course day in and day out, month in and month out, year after year. And tough as it is, that process means nothing to him because his desire to be the greatest golfer of all time is so strong.

That's what we need to find within ourselves. When we can find goals that motivate us, the process becomes insignificant. You need to be a

> **Quick Tip**
>
> Your "want" must be much stronger than the process. If so, you'll reach all your goals.

visionary and continue to consider the goal and not the process that it takes to reach that goal.

Manager Motivation

On a side note, if you're a manager reading this and you're worried about motivating other people, remember that guiding other people toward their best is a very, very difficult thing to do. A lot of gurus and trainers believe that you can't motivate another person. I don't necessarily believe that. However, the one way that I know you can't motivate others is by using fear as your motivational tool.

Motivation by fear is temporary at best and a very unsatisfying way to get things done in any case. Motivating people with a hammer instead of a carrot, whether you're a manager trying to drive results or you're a parent trying to motivate your child, is not the way to go. It's a temporary "solution," and while it may get you the immediate result that you're looking for, you can be certain it won't last.

Send messages of trust to your staff members. Give them opportunities to do the things they're good at. Allow them to make mistakes. If you do that, your employees will ooze motivation – and they'll continue to ooze motivation for the long term!

Now Take Action

List and prioritize your goals. Assess where your wants are not as strong as the process. Evaluate whether or not yours goals are real to you. Adjust them as necessary. Then take action.

Having Guts

*"A ship is safe in harbor,
but that's not what ships are for."*

William Shedd

Being able to get out of your comfort zone and do something you really don't want to do is called "having guts." Knowing what you should do and not doing it because you're afraid of leaving your comfort zone is called "being a wimp."

If you take a look at the successful people around you, you'll notice how often they are willing to go outside their comfort zones to achieve something they want. They understand that having guts is essential to being successful. It doesn't matter to them if they're comfortable or not. They just do what they have to do to go where they want to go.

Do what Others Won't Do

You've got to have the guts to do something that others won't do. If you can consistently do the things that your competitors don't do – or more likely, won't do – you will be in the top three percent of your field.

Remember, your competition sits in their comfort zones, never to leave. This presents huge opportunities for you.

Let's use an example we can all relate to: sales. For a lot of people, asking a prospect about budgets or the decision making process is very difficult. It takes guts to ask those questions.

Quick Tip

Stretch beyond your comfort zone and reach heights you've only dreamed about.

Asking tough questions is essential, though. Go beyond what's comfortable for you and ask, "Do you have a budget for this type of project?" Follow up with "Do you mind sharing it with me in round numbers?" People are not used to hearing quality questions like that. It leaves them with no option but to answer the questions. Why? Because they don't want to leave their comfort zones by telling you they can't answer your questions.

Let's take it one step further and talk about price, a pretty common obstacle that salespeople face. If you have the guts to stick to your price when someone gives you a little push back, you are going to be more successful and you're going to make more money. When we understand the value of what we offer, we won't automatically reduce price just because a customer raises an objection.

This principle can apply to any employee in any role. Just because someone pushes back on an idea or suggestion does not mean you have to cave in. Sure, you don't want to be a jerk about how you respond and butt heads with another person unnecessarily. However, having the guts to stand up for yourself and what you believe is the right thing to do. When you do that tactfully, you'll gain tremendous respect.

Finally, it also takes guts to close the sale. If you can ask for the sale consistently, when the time is right, you're going to dramatically boost your sales income. Have guts to do the things that you might be a little scared of right now – things outside your comfort zone – and success is sure to follow.

Now Take Action

How can you go outside of your comfort zone today? Is it by asking questions in a meeting, confronting someone who's done you wrong, or asking someone for help? Whatever it is, chose one and do it now. Have guts!

Killing Fear

"Fear of failure must never be a reason not to try something."

Frederick Smith

The most successful people in every profession experience fear. But the key to their success is that they know how to overcome that fear. They understand that mental toughness can overcome any obstacle. They also know that if they do the things they fear, over time that fear will no longer exist.

Successful people know that 99 percent of the time, the thing they feared is not nearly as bad as they built it up to be.

Easiest Way to Overcome Any Fear

The easiest and best way to overcome any fear is by doing one simple thing: taking action!

When you take action, fear subsides. When you get the ball rolling and momentum takes over, fear turns into power.

Have you ever been in a situation where you were afraid to ask someone a question because you were apprehensive about how they would react? For some reason, though, you asked the question anyway and got a totally different reaction than you expected. And you said to yourself, "Wow. That was easy!" You just did it – and it worked out fine.

That "just do it" men-
tality is exactly what we're
talking about here. Too
often, we talk ourselves
into crazy stuff that is so

> **Quick Tip**
>
> Do the thing you fear, and over time, that fear will no longer exist.

far from reality that it paralyzes us into inaction. We work ourselves into such a frenzy of fear that we can't even comprehend doing the thing we fear. To be successful in anything, learn to conquer fear. The best way to do it is to simply take action and disregard negative self talk.

Now Take Action

What fears do you have right now? Making a phone call to explain why something didn't work out as planned? Is it asking someone to do something they've been putting off? Choose one and take immediate action on it. You will kill your fear.

Self Awareness

"Know thyself."

Socrates

In my opinion, self awareness, though it's an essential key to success, is often overlooked. It's vital to understand what makes you tick. To understand why you do the things you do, why you make the decisions you make, and why those decisions make you feel the way they do is crucial insight.

That understanding will provide you opportunity and freedom to change the things you'd like to change about yourself and create the success you desire. Without knowing who you are, self acceptance and change become impossible.

Not understanding what drives you and not knowing why certain things affect you the way they do is like driving a car with no steering wheel. You may get to where you want to go, but you'll have no idea how you got there and it will take ten times as long.

The Best Way to Become Self Aware

The best way that I know of to eliminate all the guesswork when it comes to your self awareness is to complete a personality profile. You can go online and fill out a simple profile questionnaire to see what really motivates you. In minutes, you can see how your personality works with others and learn the best environment for you to be successful.

You can do this easily by visiting our website at www.YouCanExpectSuccess.com and clicking on the resource page, where you'll find a list of our recommended personality profile companies.

> **Quick Tip**
>
> Go online and conduct your own personality profile. This is the quickest and best way to understand more about the person you are.

Most of these personality profiles are online and are quick and inexpensive to complete. The value and the information you'll gather will be tremendously beneficial. You'll be setting yourself up for success because you're going to be able to live, work, and play in a world that is suited to you.

You will discover things about yourself that you never knew. You'll find yourself saying, "Now that makes sense!" You will gain a new understanding of what makes you the person you are. In turn, you can surround yourself with the kind of people and work environment you need to be successful.

Imagine doing something you love and enjoying your job rather than having to go to "work." Imagine taking the first steps on your lifelong career journey. Imagine how that will make you feel.

Now Take Action

I suggest reading the book, *StrengthsFinder 2.0*, by Tom Rath. Included with his book is a Web-based personality questionnaire, developed by the Gallup Organization, that will uncover your own top talents. It's an awesome tool that I have personally used.

Personal Accountability

"Personal accountability is about each of us holding ourselves accountable for our own thinking and behaviors and the results they produce."

John G. Miller

If I could sum up this entire book in two words, they would be "personal accountability."

First, let's note that we're talking about *personal* accountability, not someone else's accountability. Personal accountability is being responsible for your actions, without excuses. Personal accountability is the ability and willingness to eliminate internal attitudes like blame and finger pointing from your life.

When it comes down to it, you can achieve everything in this entire book if you take personal accountability for your actions. It comes down to simple choices. Choose not to place blame on others. Choose not to point fingers when someone fails to meet a deadline. And choose not to put off difficult tasks.

You must always remember that you are in control of your thoughts and that your thoughts control your actions. No one else makes us do the things we do – we do!

What's the difference between someone who is very successful and who achieves all her goals and you? Nothing! You can do it, too. All you need to do is decide to do it. Take personal responsibility for your results. Take action.

Once you accept personal accountability, excuses no longer exist. You'll be free from the pressure of worrying whether someone else is doing his job. Or why a colleague got a promotion. Or why someone "threw you under the bus." All of those worries cease to exist when you accept responsibility for the course of your life.

Why Don't We Practice Personal Accountability?

Whose fault is it when employees blame others for their problems? Or when they complain about other departments not doing their jobs? Or when they put off difficult tasks?

Unfortunately, most problems exist because of one simple reason:

Human nature!

It's human nature for us to blame others for our problems or to complain about things that don't meet our standards. The reason we behave this way is because we don't know any better. We fall back on the default responses that Nature has built into us. Most of us have never been taught to overcome these problems, eliminate our excuses, and adapt to change in an easy way.

> **Did You Know?**
>
> When we accept personal accountability for our actions, we eliminate blame and finger pointing from our lives.

Sure we could blame our parents. But it's not their fault. They don't know any better. The truth is that we haven't been taught the right way to truly eliminate these problems and in turn create a productive environment.

Negativity is one of the most contagious "diseases" in existence. It is so much easier to be negative towards someone than to commend them. If we disagree with someone, what do we do? We put them down! We don't see the issue from their side until after it's already turned into an argument and feelings get hurt.

As people, we're unaware of how to control these emotions on a conscious level. We behave the only way we know how, and that is to mimic and copy the behavior of the people we've been around our entire life. Unfortunately, these people have never been taught anything different, either!

For example, if a new and inexperienced employee starts work in a department where the manager is a micro manager, the only way they will learn to manage is as a micro manager themselves.

This employee will not know any better. He will just be duplicating the things that were taught to him. He has no choice.

The same thing goes for everything we do and have done in our lives.

Why Productivity Gets Destroyed

The number one reason that behaviors like blame and finger pointing are unacceptable is because they destroy the productivity, morale, and teamwork of employees.

If you don't take responsibility for your actions how can you expect to perform at a high level and achieve success? You can't. Take care of yourself first. Then and only then can you look to your Outer Circle for help.

Bottom Line

The bottom line that we're trying to get at is that all employee problems, and all personal problems for that matter, happen because of unaltered, untrained human nature.

We simply don't know any better unless we're taught a different way.

Isn't it time you found a better way?

Personal accountability is that better way. When you make the choice to be accountable for your actions, you're going to begin to develop a solution mindset. When problems arise, instead of pointing fingers and expecting others to find solutions, you're going to be able to present a solution and quickly solve problems.

Now Take Action

As I mentioned before, I am a true believer in the principle that personal accountability controls everything we do. It dictates our success.

Because personal accountability is so crucial to success, I have partnered with the leading authority on personal accountability training, John G. Miller. John is the author of *QBQ! The Question behind the Question* and the developer of a proven accountability training system for every company, regardless of industry. Visit the private website listed below and download a free report, audio CD, and online videos that demonstrate the complete QBQ! training system.

**Download your personal accountability
report, CD, and videos at:**

www.AchieveNational.com/free-info

Success Wheel Revisited

Now that you have discovered the 15 Critical Success Factors, let's complete our Success Wheel. As you might have guessed, personal accountability is our hub. It's everyone's hub. Without it, we will squirm around in mediocrity forever. With it, we can accomplish anything.

That said your Success Wheel looks like the graphic on the next page. By having a central focus on personal accountability, we can use the other Success Factors to help us accomplish goals and desires much faster. The reason for that is because once you accept 100% responsibility for your behaviors, you'll be able to take action on the other Success Factors, instead of waiting for something to happen to you or for you.

The Success Wheel - Revisited

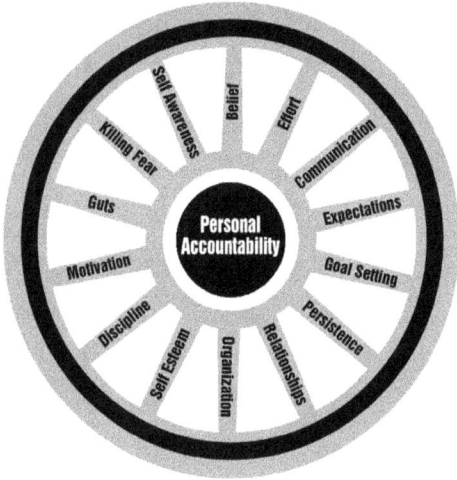

Module III

Your Success Blueprint

3

The Five-Step System

Now that you've discovered the secrets behind the Inner Circle of Success, it's time to make it work for you. Below is the simple five-step system to implementing and maximizing Inner Circle Thinking. Don't be put-off by its simplicity. That's where the magic lives.

In my experience, the easier things are to do, the more likely you'll do them and the more benefit you'll gain from doing them.

Follow these steps to help you achieve success at anything you do:

1. *When* you're struggling to accomplish something, anything, you must first ask yourself, *"What's holding me back?"*

2. Then you need to determine if it's Outer Circle Thinking (OCT) or Inner Circle Thinking (ICT). If you're focused on Outer Circle Thinking change your answer to Inner Circle Thinking. (Remember, Outer Circle Thinking is focused on things we can't control. Inner Circle Thinking is focused on things we can control.)

3. Next, change your Inner Circle Thinking statement to an Inner Circle Question (ICQ). Try starting it with, "What can I...", "How can I..." or "Where can I..."

4. Answer your ICQ. Go beyond the obvious.

5. Finally, make a plan and take action! Do something that will move you closer to accomplishing whatever it is you're trying to accomplish. Success now lies in your hands.

That's it! It's so easy to do and it works every time.

Go to *www.YouCanExpectSuccess.com/bonuses* and print out a free five-step system cheat sheet. Place it on your desk, refrigerator, mirror or anywhere else you'll see it on a regular basis.

Let's look at each step in further detail.

Step One

One of the most powerful questions you could ever ask yourself is *"What's holding me back?"* When you ask this question you will immediately begin to view your situation in a way that you haven't before. You'll start to see all the things that are standing in your way of achieving success.

The reason this question is so effective is because it's nearly impossible not to answer it honestly. You at least have an idea of what's holding you back and when you ask this question it helps bring it out so you can see it.

Step Two

For most people, when they do Step One their answers will focus on things they can't control. As you know by now this can destroy your ability to be successful. By changing your mindset to Inner Circle Thinking, only then can you start to identify the ways to gain momentum towards reaching your goals.

Step Three

The next step simply takes the result from Step Two and changes it into a question. Not any question but an Inner Circle Question. An ICQ is one that should most often start with, "What can I...", "How can I..." or "Where can I..." All you do is put the core of your Step Two results after the question prefix. For example, it might look something like, "What can I do to ensure that I exercise three times per week?" "How can I become a better teammate?" "Where can I make time to play with my kids more?"

Step Four

Now you simply answer your question. One word of caution, do not take the easy way out. Answer Step Three by going beyond the obvious. All that really means is first answer the question with whatever comes to mind. Then take a few minutes to explore some other possible answers that are not so obvious. Really dig deep and think of all the different alternatives and possibilities. By going beyond the obvious you can really discover unique solutions that will make you stand out and allow you to achieve success faster than using just the obvious answer.

Step Five

Now all you have to do is make a plan based on your answer(s) to Step Four and take action. Taking immediate action is the key. This is also were most people get bogged down. The reason for that is because their answer to Step Four may require difficult work or stretching beyond their comfort zone.

Don't fall into this trap. The easiest and best way to avoid this trap is to simply take action! Once you move forward even a little bit momentum will take over and success is earned!

Before we discuss a couple examples of this system in action I want to talk about a vital element to our success, stopping self sabotage.

Stop Self Sabotage

Many times even with the best intentions we sabotage our own efforts to be successful. Most often it occurs when we think we are focusing on our Inner Circle but for some reason we can't gain any momentum.

Below is a list of statements that appear to be focused on things we can control but see how they stop us dead in our tracks when we use them:

- "I can never do that."

- "I'm stopping. This is too hard.

- "I said no!"

- "I'll start on it tomorrow."

- "I'm not disorganized. I have an organized mess."

- "I would never join a club that would have me as a member."

- "I just don't have the discipline to accomplish that."

- "I just can't get motivated."

- "I can't ask her that!"

- "What if they think I'm stupid?"

- "I don't know what makes me tick."

As you can clearly see all of these statements do have an internal focus but they are all very negative and self-limiting.

When you find that you're making these or similar statements simply implement Step Three of the system to correct this mistake.

For example, if you want to write a book but keep saying to yourself, "I can never do that. It's a pipe-dream," change that statement into an ICQ like, "What can I do to guarantee that I get my book started?" Then, whatever the answer is to that question, take action and you're on your way to writing that book!

Do you see how powerful this is?

Now, let's look at a few examples to explain these steps further and to see where the Critical Success Factors come into play.

The Five-Step System in Action

Recently a friend of mine came to me and said he wanted to get a raise at work. He's been working hard and thought it was time.

The first thing I had him do was answer the question in Step One,: "What's holding you back?" He immediately responded with, "My boss doesn't see all the value I bring." You can see where this is headed already, can't you?

Next, after explaining Inner Circle and Outer Circle Thinking, I asked him how he could change his statement to reflect inwards, on something he can control. He started to grin and said, "I can show him the value I bring."

Of course, the next thing I asked him was to put that statement into a question. After a little help from me, he came up with, "How can I show my boss the value I bring and make it impossible for him not to give me a raise?"

As his grin turned into a wide-open, ear-to-ear, happy-go-lucky smile, he answered his own questions with statements like, "I can show him the documented error -free reports that I complete on time, every time. I can show him the perfect customer satisfaction score I have. I will even show him my perfect attendance for the last two years." He continued on for another minute or so before I said, "Do you see how you control your success?"

Another question I had to ask was, "If you're already doing this, do you know why you haven't received a raise before?" He didn't even have to think before answering, "He's too busy doing other things to notice me. But that's okay because now I know it's up to me to get noticed. And I know how to grab his attention and prove that I deserve this raise!" Needless to say, my friend is overloaded with excitement about the possibilities that lie ahead. All he has to do now is take action.

Let's now look at an example on a personal level. Something most everyone can relate to, losing weight.

Every weight loss program works. However, they are not all created equal. Frankly, a lot of the weight loss programs are simply not practical enough to fit into most people's lifestyles. You've got to find the right one for you.

With that being said, the first thing you need to do is ask yourself, "What's holding me back?" You may answer with something like, "Time. I don't have enough time to follow a program or get to the gym."

Eliminate the "Time" Excuse Forever

Time is the one and only thing that is created equal for every person on this earth. What makes one person get so much done in a day's time when another doesn't seem to get anything done? The number of answers can be infinite, depending on the situation; however, the fact remains that there are only 24 hours in a day.

From this point forward, eliminate the "time" excuse from your life. Plan your days better, get more organized, and never again say, "I don't have time."

Now that we've got that out of the way, you may answer the question from Step One with, "Every weight loss plan I've tried didn't work."

Steps Two and Three; change that OCT statement into an ICT statement, such as, "How can I find the right weight loss program for me?" It looks like you already made it into an ICQ, which is great!

Only you can answer that question. It will be different for everyone. The bottom line is that you do know the answer. And once you take action on the answer, you can't help but to be successful in your weight loss efforts.

To ensure your success even further, you don't have to stop after one ICQ. You can develop an entire list, if needed. As long as you manage the list appropriately and take action, you'll accomplish anything you desire.

This is where the 15 Critical Success Factors come into play. Keep reading to find out how.

How and Where to Use the Critical Success Factors

Continuing with the weight loss example, let's look at how the Critical Success Factors can help us further.

If you want to achieve ultimate success, add this step to the five-step system and call it "Step 4b." Here's how it works.

After you change your ICT to an ICQ, go through the entire list of success factors and develop ICQs for each.

For example, if you want to lose weight, you can ask yourself some of the following questions:

- "How can I truly <u>believe</u> that I can lose weight?"

- "What can I do to make sure I put forth the <u>effort</u> needed to lose weight?"

- "How can I develop the <u>discipline</u> I need to lose weight?"

- "How can I <u>conquer the fear</u> I have of joining a gym?"

- "How can I <u>organize</u> my schedule to make time for the gym and following my weight loss plan?"

The above examples are just five of the fifteen success factors you can use.

Can you imagine if you went through all fifteen and then took massive action? I would say with 100% certainty that you would succeed in your weight loss goals.

Think for a second about other goals you want to accomplish. How much more effective are you going to be in achieving them when you go through this process?

No one said achieving success was going to be easy. After all, that's why one of the Critical Success Factors is 'effort.'

You can accomplish anything you want by following this system and incorporating the 15 Critical Success Factors. It's your choice to use and implement the system.

This System Creates Motivation

When you start to use this five-step success system, you will immediately notice an increase in motivation and a strong "want" to get things done. That's what this system does. It demands that you take action. Action turns into motion, motion turns into momentum, and momentum turns into results.

Each step of this system is equally important. They build off one another. You can't skip straight to Step Four without completing the previous three steps.

Following each step in order is like a small snowball at the top of a mountain that starts rolling down. As the snowball gets bigger and bigger, it gains momentum and goes faster and faster until it is an unstoppable force.

Implement this five-step system and you'll be an unstoppable force and achieve success in everything you do.

Integrity of Your Inner Circle

If you're like a lot of people who read this book, you might be saying to yourself, "There's more than 15 Success Factors. What about honesty, integrity, and gratitude?" If that's crossed your mind, you'd be right in saying that. Certainly, these fifteen success factors are not all encompassing. But they are absolutely the most critical to your ongoing success.

Most everything successful people do depends on one or more of these 15 Critical Success Factors. For everything else, that's where the "Integrity of your Inner Circle" comes in.

In short, the Integrity of your Inner Circle means understanding the difference between right and wrong. If you're following the five-step system, and it feels "right," it probably is, resulting in Inner Circle Thinking.

However, if something doesn't feel right, but you can't pinpoint exactly why, it's most likely a byproduct of Outer Circle Thinking. For example, if your answer to "What's holding me back?" starts with "I wish..." or "I want...," you will violate the Integrity of Your Inner Circle. You're still focused on Outer Circle Thinking, even though you've used the word "I".

Let's say you're trying to be more successful with your kids, and you answer Step 1 with, "I want my kids to listen better." or "I wish my kids would do what they're told." Statements like these clearly violate the integrity of your Inner Circle because they are focused on things beyond your control. I want you to take a second right now and repeat those statements out loud. Go ahead. Now, don't they just feel wrong?

When you take into account the Integrity of your Inner Circle in everything you do, it won't matter if it relates to one of the fifteen success factors or not. You'll be setting yourself up to succeed because you'll be making better choices and better decisions automatically. It will just feel better.

Living with H.I.P.E.

I like to think of the Integrity of your Inner Circle with the acronym, H.I.P.E. It's pronounced, "hype," but it certainly has a much different meaning. HIPE stands for Honesty, Integrity, Passion, Everyday.

When you put the word "living with" in front of HIPE, you get the true essence of what Inner Circle Thinking is all about.

When you live your life with honesty, integrity, and passion every day, and combine that with the 15 Critical Success Factors and add in your new found skill of Inner Circle Thinking, is there any possible way you can't achieve all the success you can handle? Of course not.

So get after it and achieve all your dreams!

Closing Thoughts

First, let me congratulate you on reading this book. I'm sure you'll agree that by taking action on what you learned, you will dramatically boost performance and achievement.

By following this information, you will enhance your professional career as well as your personal life. You're going to feel a tremendous amount of energy because your confidence will be at an all-time high and you'll achieve things you never thought possible.

Now Take Action

Now that you know what it takes to be successful, isn't it time you shared this information with others?

In the Action Guide at the back of this book, you'll find information on how you can order copies of this book for your employees, colleagues, family, and friends.

You'll also discover a private club for readers of this book. Ideally, this club is for people who want that extra motivation every month. We call it our "Audio-of-the-Month Club."

Do yourself a favor and join today!

> To order additional copies of
> *Expect Success*, please visit:
>
> **www.YouCanExpectSuccess.com**
>
> or use the form in the back of this book.

About the Author

Drew Laughlin is widely considered to be one of the leading authorities on performance development.

Drew has helped organizations eliminate internal problems while maximizing productivity and achievement. He has operated two successful corporate training programs, one with a focus on personal accountability and the second on sales and marketing training. He now offers corporate training and consulting and coaching services.

When he's not working, Drew spends time with his family (wife, Debbie, and kids, Taylor and Sam), watching sports, especially college football, or out on the golf course.

Visit one of Drew's sites today:

- YouCanExpectSuccess.com
- AchieveNational.com
- DrewLaughlin.com

Action Guide

Success Tips and Strategies

Visit YouCanExpectSuccess.com today and get your:

- Free success newsletter
- Free reports
- Free audio downloads
- Free online videos
- Free success tips and strategies
- Online courses
- Other useful tools to help you reach the pinnacle of success

Share *Expect Success* with Others

Use the form at the back of this book to order additional copies of Expect Success for your employees, colleagues, family, and friends.

Quantity discounts are available.

Enjoy!

Expect Success

Audio-of-the-Month Club

Want to maximize your success? Why not join our Audio-of–the-Month Club?

Every month, you'll receive a new audio master class in downloadable MP3 format, complete with PDF transcripts, from top experts on improving and developing critical performance skills. This program is perfect for:

- Self study programs
- Lunch-and-learns
- Your personal resource library
- Listening in your car on the way to work/appointments
- Reducing training expenses

How It Works

1. Go to www.YouCanExpectSuccess.com/audio and sign up today. NOTE: This is a fixed-term club that only lasts for a specific period of time.
2. Every month you will receive the "Audio-of-the-Month" delivered to your email inbox. You will receive access to a private Web page where you can download the MP3 version with PDF transcripts.
3. You can cancel any time.
4. You're protected by our money back guarantee. If you aren't satisfied with your first month's audio master class, let us know and you'll receive a full refund!

Join today!

www.YouCanExpectSuccess.com/audio

Two Easy Ways to Order

Expect Success

PHONE
Call 402.682.2825
Customer Service Hours:
8:00 a.m. – 5:00 p.m., M-F

WEBSITE
www.YouCanExpectSuccess.com/book
Visit us online, 24/7

Pricing

1-9	For quantities of 1-9 please place book orders at Amazon.com ($10.95 each)
10-49	$10.45 each
50-99	$9.95 each
100-500	$8.95 each
500 or more	$7.95 each

Shipping is $4.00, plus 6.25% of book total. Orders are shipped ground delivery and will arrive in seven to ten business days.

Questions?
Call us today at 402-682-2625

Thank you for your support!

www.ingramcontent.com/pod-product-compliance
Lightning Source LLC
Chambersburg PA
CBHW060044210326
41520CB00009B/1252